POEMS ABOUT BEING BORN
AND GROWING OLDER

ME!

CHOSEN BY WENDY COOLING

Illustrated by Rowan Barnes-Murphy

FRANKLIN WATTS
NEW YORK • LONDON • SYDNEY

First published in 2000 by Franklin Watts
96, Leonard Street, London EC2A 4XD

Franklin Watts Australia
14 Mars Road, Lane Cove, NSW 2066

© in this anthology Wendy Cooling 2000
Illustrations © Rowan Barnes-Murphy 2000

Editor: Sarah Snashall
Designer: Louise Thomas
Art director/cover design: Jonathan Hair
Border artwork: Diana Mayo

A CIP catalogue record for this book
is available from the British Library.

ISBN 0 7496 3482 0

Dewey classification 821.008

Printed in Hong Kong/China

Acknowledgments

The editor and publishers gratefully acknowledge
permission to reproduce the following copyright material.

Copy, by Richard Armour. Reprinted by permission of
Heinemann Educational. *Newborn Child,* by Norman
Silver. © Norman Silver 1994, *The Walkman Have Landed*
(Faber and Faber). Permission granted by the author. *Baby
Brother,* by Jonathan Shipton. Reprinted by permission of
the author. *The Baby of the Family,* by Wendy Cope.
Reprinted by permission of the author. *One,* by James
Berry, from *When I Dance* (Puffin). Reprinted by
permission of The Peters Fraser and Dunlop Group
Limited on behalf of James Berry. *Bodies,* by Gina
Douthwaite, from *Word Whirls,* ed. John Foster (OUP,
1998). *Biking,* by Judith Nicholls. © Judith Nicholls 1987.
From *Midnight Forest,* published by Faber and Faber.
Reprinted by permission of the author. *First Day at
School,* by Roger McGough, from *In the Glassroom*
(Cape). Reprinted by permission of The Peters Fraser and
Dunlop Group Limited on behalf of Roger McGough.
Picking Teams, by Allan Ahlberg, from *Please Mrs Butler,*
by Allan Ahlberg (Kestrel, 1983). © Allan Ahlberg, 1983.
Reprinted by permission of Penguin Books Ltd.
Arithmetic, by Carl Sandburg, from *The Complete Poems
of Carl Sandburg.* © 1970, 1969 by Lilian Steichen
Sandburg, Trustee. Reprinted by permission of Harcourt,
Inc. *People,* by Charlotte Zolotow. © 1967, renewed
© 1995 by Charlotte Zolotow. Reprinted by permission of
Scott Treimel New York. *Why Did You Call Me Percy?* by
Gareth Owen. © Gareth Owen, 1994. Reproduced by
permission of the author c/o Rogers, Coleridge & White
Ltd., 20 Powis Mews, London W11 1JN. *All You Want to
Do,* by Julie O'Callaghan. Reprinted by permission of the
author. *Change,* by Charlotte Zolotow. © 1970 by
Charlotte Zolotow. Reprinted by permission of Scott
Treimel New York. *Childhood,* by Francis Cornford.
Reprinted by the permission of the F. Cornford Estate. *On
Ageing,* by Maya Angelou. From *And Still I Rise,* by Maya
Angelou. Reprinted by permission of Virago Press.
Grandad, by Kit Young. From *Rabbiting On,* by Kit
Young. Reprinted by permission of the author. *Thinking
About the Future,* by Jenny Joseph. From *Dear Future… A
Time Capsule of Poems,* ed. David Orme (Hodder).
Reprinted by permission of the author.

Every effort has been made to trace copyright, but if any
omissions have been made please let us know in order that
we may put it right in the next edition.

CONTENTS

COPY

His mother's eyes,
His father's chin.
His auntie's nose,
His uncle's grin,

His great-aunt's hair,
His grandma's ears,
His grandpa's mouth,
So it appears...

Poor little tot,
Well may he moan.
He hasn't much
To call his own.

by Richard Armour

NEWBORN CHILD

I am not a Buddhist,
I am not Hindu,
  I am not a Muslim –
    but I'm just like you.

    Just like you –
    and you're just like me,
    inside there are no differences
    for us to see.

    I am not a Christian,
    I am not a Jew,
    I am not a Heathen –
    but I'm just like you.

Just like you –
and you're just like me,
and there isn't any simpler way
for us to be.

by Norman Silver

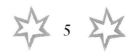

BABY BROTHER
(for Dylan)

The baby wakes
The baby sleeps
The baby squeaks for weeks
And weeks.

The baby crawls
The baby creeps
The baby trips
And sprawls
And weeps.

The baby dribbles
The baby spits
The baby breaks
Your toys to bits!

The baby bites
And pulls your hair
He wants to follow
Everywhere!

The baby wants to be your friend

The baby
Drives you
Round The Bend!

by Jonathan Shipton

THE BABY OF THE FAMILY

Up on Daddy's shoulders
He is riding high –
The baby of the family,
A pleased, pork pie.
I'm tired and my feet are sore –
It seems all wrong.
He's lucky to be little
But it won't last long.

The baby of the family,
He grabs my toys
And when I grab them back he makes
A big, loud noise.
I mustn't hit him, so I chant
This short, sweet song:
"You're lucky to be little
But it won't last long."

Everybody looks at him
And thinks he's sweet,
Even when he bellows "No!"
And stamps his feet.
He won't be so amusing
When he's tall and strong.
It's lovely being little
But it won't last long.

by Wendy Cope

ONE

Only one of me
and nobody can get a second one
from a photocopy machine.

Nobody has the fingerprints I have.
Nobody can cry my tears, or laugh my laugh
or have my expectancy when I wait.

But anybody can mimic my dance with my dog.
Anybody can howl how I sing out of tune.
And mirrors can show me multiplied
many times, say, dressed up in red
or dressed up in grey.

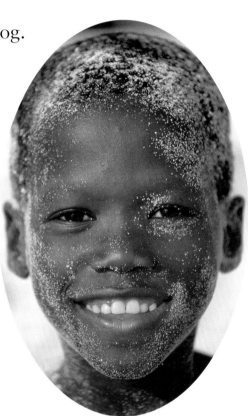

Nobody can get into my clothes for me
or feel my fall for me, or do my running.
Nobody hears my music for me, either.

I am just this one.
Nobody else makes the words
I shape with sound, when I talk.

But anybody can act how I stutter in a rage.
Anybody can copy echoes I make.
And mirrors can show me multiplied
many times, say, dressed up in green
or dressed up in blue.

by James Berry

BODIES

Bodies are
blood, brains
and bones,
tubes that
loop
and
chromosomes,
organs, gastro-gases, guts, veins and valves,
and glands
with ducts,
fluids, flesh,
fat, feet,
and
fingers,
held in shape
(that's what the
skin does)

s   T
o   h
         a
t   t
h   's
e
y   w
         h
a   y
l
l   b
         o
l   d
o   i
o   e
k   s
m
u   n
c   e
h   e
         d
t
h   a
e
same.   name.   *by Gina Douthwaite*

9

FIRST DAY AT SCHOOL

A millionbillionwillion miles from home
Waiting for the bell to go. (To go where?)
Why are they all so big, other children?
So noisy? So much at home they
must have been born in uniform
Lived all their lives in playgrounds
Spent the years inventing games
that don't let me in. Games
that are rough, that swallow you up.

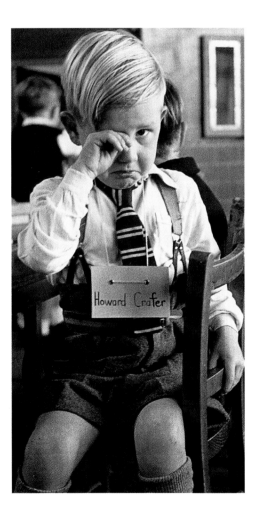

And the railings.
All around, the railings.
Are they to keep out wolves and monsters?
Things that carry off and eat children?
Things you don't take sweets from?
Perhaps they're to stop us getting out
Running away from the lessins. Lessin.
What does a lessin look like?
Sounds small and slimy.
They keep them in glassrooms.
Whole rooms made out of glass. Imagine.

I wish I could remember my name
Mummy said it would come in useful.
Like wellies. When there's puddles.
Yellowwellies. I wish she was here.
I think my name is sewn on somewhere
Perhaps the teacher will read it for me.
Tea-cher. The one who makes the tea.

by Roger McGough

BIKING

Fingers grip,
toes curl;
head down,
wheels whirl.

Hair streams,
fields race;
ears sting,
winds chase.

Breathe deep,
troubles gone;
just feel
windsong.

by Judith Nicholls

PICKING TEAMS

When we pick teams in the playground,
Whatever the game might be,
There's always somebody left till last
And usually it's me.

I stand there looking hopeful
And tapping myself on the chest,
But the captains pick the others first,
Starting, of course, with the best.

Maybe, if teams were sometimes picked
Starting with the worst,
Once in his life a boy like me
Could end up being first!

by Allan Ahlberg

ARITHMETIC

Arithmetic is where numbers fly like pigeons in and out of
      your head.
Arithmetic tells you how many you lose or win if you know
      how many you had before you lost or won.
Arithmetic is seven eleven all good children go to heaven –
      or five six bundle of sticks.
Arithmetic is numbers you squeeze from your head to your
      hand to your pencil to your paper till you get the answer.
Arithmetic is where the answer is right and everything is
      nice and you can look out of the window and see the blue
      sky – or the answer is wrong and you have to start all over
      again and try again and see how it comes out this time.
If you take a number and double it and double it again and
      then double it a few more times, the number gets bigger
      and bigger and goes higher and higher and only arithmetic
      can tell you what the number is when you decide to
      quit doubling.
Arithmetic is where you have to multiply – and you carry the
      multiplication table in your head and hope you won't lose
      it.
If you have two animal crackers, one good and one bad,
      and you eat one and a striped zebra with streaks all over
      him eats the other, how many animal crackers will you
      have if somebody offers you five six seven and you say No
      no no and you say Nay nay nay and you say Nix nix nix?
If you ask your mother for one fried egg for breakfast and
      she gives you two fried eggs and you eat both of them,
      who is better in arithmetic, you or your mother?

by Carl Sandburg

TIGER

There should be a tiger in every book,
  And just as you're having to sit and look
At eight and one and three times two
 And how many's left if I give four to you,
  Growling and padding
  Straight through the print—
  Golden as sunshine,
  Striped like a mint—
  The tiger comes stalking
  Across the page.
 Not in a circus,
 Not in a cage,
  But wandering freely
   Right out of the book—
   As you sit there amazed
   With a dumbfounded look—
  Scattering numbers,
Terrifying words
Like dozens of tiny black fluttering birds,
Until he strides majestically proud
Across desks and tables, growling aloud
And sits on the blackboard working his jaws,
Idly licking the chalk off his paws.
 And then at last, looking grandly about,
  He dissolves in the blackboard
   As Miss rubs him out.

by Joan Guest

14

HILL ROLLING

I kind of exploded inside,
and joy shot out of me.
I began to roll down the grassy hill.
I bent my knees up small, took a
        deep breath
and I was off.
My arms shot out sideways.
I gathered speed.
My eyes squinted
Sky and grass, dazzle and dark.

I went on forever,
My arms were covered with dents,
holes, squashed grass.
Before I knew it I was at the bottom.
The game was over.
The door of the classroom closed behind me.
I can smell chalk dust, and hear the voice of teacher,
to make me forget my hill.

by Andrew Taylor

BE LIKE THE BIRD

Be like the bird, who
Resting in his flight
On a twig too slight
Feels it bend beneath him,
Yet sings
Knowing he has wings.

by Victor Hugo

THE GIRL FOOTBALLER

No one called the Girl Footballer's name,
even when she played a great game.
Not even when she scored a hat-trick –
nutmeg, lob, scissor kick –

Did anyone shout the Girl Footballer's name?
Her talent was like a burning flame.
Why was it? Who was to blame?
That no one called the Girl Footballer's name.

The boys in her very own team,
never bothered to find out her name.
They'd shout: "Oi! Over here!
Pass it! Boot it! It's clear!"

The Girl Footballer did a cunning dummy.
A lush lob, scored a double whammy.
She marked her man like glue.
She could dribble rings round you.

Chip, scissor kick, volley, curl –
the Girl Footballer was some girl.
Whack it. Head it. Shoot it. Boot it.
Football was her thrill.

Soon she had admirers.
From far and wide they came to watch her flying headers.
The crowd for the Girl grew and grew.
One fan found out her name was Su.

Next match, she scored a winning goal,
nutmegged the goalie.
For the first time, a hug from a boy.
You should have seen Su jump for joy.

Suddenly every fan started shouting her name,
as the Girl Footballer's shot clinched the game.
And her own team look silly and tame,
until they too shouted the Girl Footballer's name.

...Eh-Eh Eeee Oh, Go-Su-go. Go-Su-go.

by Jackie Kay

 17

FIRST DATE

When you race home from school,
    With your hair all askew,
You've loads of revision,
    And homework to do,
When all that is finished,
    You shampoo your hair,
Then dry it, and style it,
    With slow loving care,
You've barely got time,
    For a quick bite to eat,
Before you can change,
    Into something quite neat,
But it's got to look modern,
    And feminine too,
Then when you've changed,
    There's your make-up to do,
And now that your face,
    Is looking just right,
You glance in the mirror,
    Wow! what a sight!
He'll never resist you,
    You don't think he'll try,
Your heart beats loudly,
    Your spirits run high,
You look out the window,
    He's there at the gate,
And you hurry downstairs,
    To your very first date.

by Susan Whyte

PEOPLE

Some people talk and talk
and never say a thing.
Some people look at you
and birds begin to sing.

Some people laugh and laugh
and yet you want to cry.
Some people touch your hand
and music fills the sky.

by Charlotte Zolotow

☆ 19 ☆

COLOURED

When I was born, I was black.
When I grew up, I was black.
When I get hot, I am black.
When I get cold, I am black.
When I am sick, I am black.
When I die, I am black.

When you were born, You were pink.
When you grew up, You were white.
When you get hot, You go red.
When you get cold, You go blue.
When you are sick, You go purple.
When you die, You go green.

AND YET YOU HAVE THE CHEEK TO CALL ME
COLOURED!!!

Anon. U5Z, King Edward VI School, Handsworth, Birmingham, UK

ME

You got no right
to look at me,
There might be things
I don't want you to see.
Things I need
to hide
behind this mask,
my face.

by Deepak Kalha

WHY DID YOU CALL ME PERCY?

Dad, why did you call me Percy?
Why did you give me that name?
I only have to think of it
And I go puce with shame.
Mum, why did you call me Percy?
It's a name that no one would want
Did you suffer some kind of brainstorm
When you named me at the font?
What was wrong with David
Or Fred or Wayne or Sam
Or any other kind of name
That sounds like what I am?
Percy sounds like someone
Who helps his mother cook
Brings apples for the teacher
Presses flowers in a book.
Who goes skipping through the countryside
Or keeps a budgie for a pet
Who cries when soap gets in his eyes
Or when his feet get wet.
I'd love to be something like Conan
Or someone with a name like Keith
Who sings and dances on the stage
And plays guitars with his teeth.
And what was wrong with Eddie
Or Rod or Cliff or Rick
Or Jimmy, Ben or Phil or Geoff
Or Elvis, John or Mick?

But Percy, stupid Percy
It goes through me like a knife
Did you never think when you called me that
He'd be with me all my life?

by Gareth Owen

ALL YOU WANT TO DO

Someday you will tell your mother,
    "So sorry – I don't want to visit
    the children's art exhibit."
To your father you will explain,
    "If you don't mind, I'll give that
    young person's concert a miss."
When the doorbell rings, say,
    "Thanks anyway, but I'm not in the mood
    for pancakes and kite-flying."
Supposing your friend invites you, reply,
    "There's no ice-skating and doughnuts
    for me today – maybe I can go next week."
If it's your cousin on the phone, try,
    "Have fun at the movies,
    don't throw popcorn at the screen."

        All you want to do
        is sit in the kitchen
        twirling spaghetti
        onto a fork
        and after that
        stop at the window
        as if watching for snow.

by Julie O'Callaghan

CHANGE

The summer
still hangs
heavy and sweet
with sunlight
as it did last year.

The autumn
still comes
showering gold and crimson
as it did last year.

The winter
still stings
clean and cold and white
as it did last year.

The spring
still comes
like a whisper in the dark night.

It is only I
who have changed.

by Charlotte Zolotow

YOUTH AND AGE

Impatient of his childhood,
     "Ah me!" exclaimed young Arthur,
Whilst roving in the wild wood,
     "I wish I were my father!"
Meanwhile, to see his Arthur
     So skip, and play, and run,
"Ah me!" exclaims the father,
     "I wish I were my son!"

by Thomas Hood

CHILDHOOD

I used to think that grown-up people chose
To have stiff backs and wrinkles round their nose,
And veins like small fat snakes on either hand,
On purpose to be grand.
Till through the banisters I watched one day
My great-aunt Etty's friend who was going away,
And how her onyx beads had come unstrung.
I saw her grope to find them as they rolled;
And then I knew that she was helplessly old,
And I was helplessly young.

by Francis Cornford

ONLY THE MOON

When I was a child I thought
The new moon was a cradle
The full moon was granny's round face.

The new moon was a banana
The full moon was a big cake.

When I was a child
I never saw the moon
I only saw what I wanted to see.

And now I see the moon
It's the moon
Only the moon, and nothing but the moon.

by Wong May, translated by E. Thumboo

27

ON AGEING

When you see me sitting quietly,
Like a sack left on the shelf,
Don't think I need your chattering.
I'm listening to myself.
Hold! Stop! Don't pity me!
Hold! Stop you sympathy!
Understanding if you got it,
Otherwise I'll do without it!

When my bones are stiff and aching
And my feet won't climb the stair,
I will only ask one favour:
Don't bring me no rocking chair.

When you see me walking, stumbling,
Don't study and get it wrong.
'Cause tired don't mean lazy
And every goodbye ain't gone.
I'm the same person I was back then,
A little less hair, a little less chin,
A lot less lungs and much less wind.
But ain't I lucky I can still breathe in.

by Maya Angelou

28

GRANDAD

Grandad's dead
And I'm sorry about that.

He'd a huge black overcoat.
He felt proud in it.
You could have hidden
A football crowd in it.
Far too big –
It was a lousy fit
But Grandad didn't
Mind a bit.
He wore it all winter
With a squashed black hat.

Now he's dead
And I'm sorry about that.

He'd got twelve stories.
I'd heard every one of them
Hundreds of times
But that was the fun of them:
You knew what was coming
So you could join in.
He'd got big hands
And brown, grooved skin
And when he laughed
It knocked you flat.

Now he's dead
And I'm sorry about that.

by Kit Wright

THINKING ABOUT THE FUTURE

When I am old, and the world is very old,
Will there be puddles?
– Puddles that reflect the sky
Puddles for us to splash through
Emptying them out, muddying them?

I expect so.

Will there be ice cream and treats?
Will there be parties and combing my hair and
    putting best clothes on
Will there be birthdays and presents and shopping
    for presents?
And who will be there?

That I don't know. I don't know.
But I hope so.

Will there be houses and gardens and toys in a cupboard
And babies to look after and doctors for when you're ill?
Will there be holidays and games on the beach and uncles
    and aunts?
And food and 'fridges to fill?

It may be so.

Will there be stories and books and people who can read
    what you're writing?
When I am old will there be children who ask me to read
And tell them stories to stop me being cross when they
    squabble?

Well, if you learn to read and write and teach your children
Let us hope so.

Will there be an end to time and a great huge fire
That burns all the streets and the houses and we fall into a pit?
And shall I be burnt and there be nothing to eat
And no animals or pets or school, or water and parents even?

That I don't know, I don't know,
But before it happens
Shall we go out now while we can
And play in the snow?

If there are people there in the future, grown-ups and children,
Will they have boots for the snow? Will they be allowed
To stay up late? What will they do?
And what will they be thinking?

I don't know what will happen, but if there are people at all
You can be fairly certain that they'll be wondering about the past.

Will they be thinking about me?

Maybe. What do you want for tea?

by Jenny Joseph

INDEX OF FIRST LINES

Picture credits

Cover image and title page:
Tony Stone (Michael Busselle)

Inside images:
Franklin Watts p.4 (Steve Shott);
Getty Images p.10;
Image Bank pp.5 (Elaine Sulle),
6 (Janet Delaney), 15 (Tim
Ridley), 25 (Vicky Kasala);
Images Colour Library pp. 8, 11,
21 (Lee Frost);
Magnum p.26;
Panos Pictures 18 (Paul Quayle);
Tony Stone pp. 16 (Lori Adamski
Peek), 28 (Daniel Bosler).